Divorce Secrets:

*Avoiding the Top 7 Mistakes
That Can Cost You, Your Children,
Your Assets, and Your Rights*

Vincent W. Davis

©2015 Law Offices of Vincent W. Davis & Associates

All Rights Reserved. No part of this book may be used or reproduced in any manner whatsoever without written permission of the author.

ISBN-13: 978-1543046151
ISBN-10: 1543046150

DISCLAIMER

This publication is intended to be informational only. No legal advice is being given, and no attorney-client relationship is intended to be created by reading this material. If you are facing legal issues, whether criminal or civil, seek professional legal counsel to get your questions answered.

Law Offices of Vincent W. Davis & Associates
150 N. Santa Anita Ave., Ste. 200
Arcadia, CA 91006

1-888-888-6582

Offices in:

Arcadia	Beverly Hills	Irvine
La Mirada	Long Beach	Los Angeles
Ontario	Riverside	Woodland Hills

Contents

1. Avoiding Costly Mistakes 9
2. Mistake 1: Choosing an Attorney Without Enough Experience 10
3. Mistake 2: Timing & Trust 14
4. Mistake 3: Not Knowing Where to Look 17
5. Mistake 4: Not Knowing What You Want 19
6. Mistake 5: Low Cost = High Risk 21
7. Mistake 6: Not Using an Attorney 24
8. Mistake 7: Forgetting You're the Client 27
9. Peace of Mind from the Law Offices of Vincent W. Davis and Associates 31

Avoiding Costly Mistakes

Divorce. Separation. End of a relationship.

Whether you're married or living together, whether you have children or not, whether you're considering separation, already separated, or even already divorced, you're going through one of the most difficult things anyone can go through.

Unfortunately, for many people this experience is far worse than it should be.

They lose their children. They lose their assets. They lose their quality of life.

Because, they didn't have the right person looking out for them. They chose the wrong family law attorney.

It wasn't their fault. Maybe they trusted the wrong person. Maybe they got bad advice. Or maybe they just didn't have the information they needed. It's easy to make a wrong decision when you don't have the right information.

And there's a lot of information that goes into this decision. Not just information about the attorney. Information about you. There are many questions to ask yourself before you ask an attorney even one.

What are your expectations? Your needs? Your challenges?

People who go into this process without the right information…about themselves or their attorney…make mistakes that can cost them dearly for the rest of their lives.

That's why the Law Offices of Vincent W. Davis and Associates put together this consumer guide, so you don't go into this process blindly. So you can make informed decisions.

And avoid the mistakes that can cost you your children, your assets, and your rights.

Mistake 1: Choosing an Attorney Without Enough Experience

"How long have you been doing this?"

That's an important question to ask whenever you're hiring someone who will provide a professional service. But it may be THE most important question when you're choosing a family law attorney.

This is one of the most complicated areas of law. Especially, here in California.

There are laws, laws within laws, guidelines, loopholes…and they change constantly. More importantly…with experience, you gain knowledge. When a lawyer has practiced certain types of cases for a number of years, certain patterns emerge.

They know where to look for hidden assets. They know which questions to ask, during a deposition or at a trial. Their instincts get better. They recognize an opportunity and know how to take advantage of it.

In other words, they do a better job of fighting for their clients.

And it isn't just having experience….it's having the right type of experience. Sometimes, people turn to the attorney they've used for years, or a family friend. But if those attorneys don't specialize in family law, no matter how experienced they are, they just won't be able to do as good a job as possible for their clients.

Look at it this way….your doctor is a general practitioner who can take care of many illnesses and issues. But if you have heart trouble, you see a cardiologist. If you break your leg, you see an orthopedic surgeon. They're specialists. Family law is a specialty too.

Here's another important question to ask about experience: "Have you handled many trials?"

Trial experience is a valuable asset even when a case isn't going to trial. It helps a seasoned attorney when negotiating a settlement...financial or custody. An attorney without much courtroom experience doesn't want to go to trial against one who does. That gives the experienced attorney a big edge in negotiations.

It also helps in the investigative stage of the case. Asking the right questions and seeing how they're answered....or not answered....can result in critical and valuable information, and a big advantage to one side in the case.

You'll find all these types of experience at the Law Offices of Vincent W. Davis and Associates. Vince Davis has more than 28 years of experience as an attorney. His courtroom experience includes personally handling more than 200 family law trials. His extensive legal education includes graduating from the Trial Lawyers College. Not many family law attorneys can say that. Vince's comfort level in the courtroom has provided comfort to many clients.

Trial experience doesn't just mean you're good at arguing a case or talking to a jury. It also makes you a good listener, which is important...because, how someone answers a question...what they say and what their body language says...can be critical to a case.

Listening is a big part of our consultations with clients.

And that can make a big difference.

Vince had a client who was facing an accusation that would have cost him custody of his children if proven true. After not one or two, but five or six interviews, the client remembered a key fact…there were witnesses whose testimony changed everything. As a result, the case was won, and the client didn't lose his children. A less experienced attorney never would have gotten that information.

Experience matters.

The right type of experience matters just as much.

Mistake 2: Timing & Trust

In a divorce case, the "when" can be almost as important as the "what." Once you've decided to separate, timing becomes critical.

First of all, when do you contact an attorney? The answer is simple...the sooner, the better.

You need someone looking out for your interests. You need someone on your side.

Let's start with the separation itself. When does it become official? When is it a legal separation?

Sometimes a difference of just a few months can cost people huge sums of money. Many times, couples disagree over when the separation happened. The husband might say he moved out three years ago, and the wife might say they just decided to separate three months ago.

And if there's no legal documentation, it becomes "he said, she said"...and that's when things get tricky. Separating doesn't just mean someone moves out of the house. In fact, some couples actually still live together after becoming legally separated.

But it still comes down to the actual date of separation. Here's why that's so important. Money.

People's financial situations change. An investment pays off. Real estate goes up in value. Someone gets an inheritance or wins a lawsuit. Maybe even wins the lottery.

They might think that windfall is theirs and theirs alone…but if the legal separation date doesn't back them up, guess what becomes community property?

The same works in reverse. Their house drops in value. They lose their job. They have an accident or lose a lawsuit. They go into debt. And often an unsuspecting spouse ends up sharing the cost.

One of the reasons people get burned this way is they trust the wrong person - their spouse. That's right, the one who's divorcing them. We hear it all the time. One spouse convinces the other to use the same attorney or just a paralegal or just do it themselves "to save money". That can be a convincing argument when you're looking at a dramatic change in your lifestyle, and you're worried about having enough money to get by.

But ask yourself this. Do both parties have the same goals? - the same objectives?

Most divorces are adversarial. Each side has its own agenda. When one spouse says "let's use this as our separation date", the other spouse had better be sure it's the right one.

At the Law Offices of Vincent W. Davis and Associates, we've seen too many people come to us after they've been burned. Unfortunately, then it's too late. Once legal documents are signed and sealed, you can't turn back the clock.

Fortunately, there are others we've caught in time. Take the client who had used a paralegal and they used the date his wife said they separated. But he had moved out five years earlier and considered that their separation date. During those five years, he won a lawsuit for $800,000. If we hadn't caught that error, he could be out $400,000.

Ronald Reagan might have said it best. Trust, but verify.

Mistake 3: Not Knowing Where to Look

Show me the money!

It's easy to ask, but it isn't easy to get answers. And sometimes it isn't easy to ask either. Finances can be the most difficult aspect of any family law case.

It can be confusing, contentious, intimidating…and nasty. Money has caused spouses and partners to stop talking to each other or accuse each other of deceptive and even criminal acts. It has caused parents to use children as hostages. It has caused longtime family-owned businesses to go out of business. It can get ugly . . . very ugly.

Assets get hidden. Joint accounts get emptied. Property gets sold.

We've all heard horror stories about people who were deceived, duped…..and devastated. People who've gone from a comfortable life….even a luxurious one….to near poverty. Who struggle to support themselves and their children while a former spouse or partner lives the high-life.

It happens too often....and it often happens because the attorney they chose couldn't uncover everything. That attorney might not have known what questions to ask, or might not have known what to do with the answers.

Even when you get the financial documents you need, interpreting them can be challenging. Financial investigations are difficult and complicated. It takes special expertise and knowledge to make sure you've uncovered everything there is and are getting honest answers to your questions. Most attorneys just don't have that knowledge.

Some attorneys have people on their staff who do have the knowledge...or they farm it out...but, many just go it alone. And their clients suffer.

That specialized knowledge is one of the things that makes Vincent Davis stand out. He's actually a former Certified Public Accountant. He's trained in auditing. So he knows how to follow the money trail.

It's helped him get the best settlement possible for his clients. Alimony that's fair; child support that covers their expenses; evenly dividing family businesses and other business assets.

Vince can be a bulldog in the courtroom and a watchdog when it comes to finances. Whichever attorney you choose for your case, make sure it's one who can find what's there and get you your share.

Mistake 4: Not Knowing What You Want

What do you want? What are you looking for? What's your best-case scenario?

You can ask it different ways, but it comes down to the same thing. What do you really want out of your family law case? What do you want financially? Alimony, child support, the house, part of the business? What type of lifestyle do you want to lead? What do you want concerning your children? Full custody? Primary custody? Every weekend?

It's hard to believe, but many people don't ask themselves those questions. Even harder to believe, many family law attorneys never ask them of their clients. They tell their clients what they can expect. Sometimes circumstances in a marriage or relationship lead to lower expectations.

In cases like that, many attorneys tell their clients to be realistic, not optimistic. Too many times, clients have heard their lawyer say this: "Here's the best I think we can do". So, they believe that. So, that's all they ask for. And they consider themselves lucky to get that.

But many times, they end up with less than that...because let's face it, where you start in negotiations isn't always where you end up.

What do you want now....and what do you want in the future? That's something else many lawyers don't ask nearly enough.

Because the fact is lives change. Expenses change. Kids grow up and go to college. People retire. A settlement that seems fair today might be woefully inadequate five years down the road. It all starts with this simple but complicated question: what do you want? That's a question Vince Davis asks every one of his clients.

And, you know what many of them say? "No one has ever asked me that before. I've never thought about what I really wanted."

But isn't that what it all comes down to? No one wants to just get by, or settle...we want the best we can get for ourselves and our children. It's a family attorney's job to get that. Many don't do their job. Vince Davis does.

He may not be 100% successful all the time. But his track record is pretty good. And most of his clients come out of their cases with more than they expected going in. Here's one example of why it matters.

A professional athlete thought the best he could get was alternate weekends with his young child. But, what he really wanted was 50-50 custody. And that's what he got, even though he lives part of the year in another state, where his team plays. Not everyone is going to get everything they want. But your attorney shouldn't hold you back.

Your attorney should fight for you.

Mistake 5: Low Cost = High Risk

You can't miss the commercials on TV, radio, or the billboards - all advertising low-cost attorneys - lawyers who will take your case and won't charge you an arm and a leg. It's tempting.

After all, your life is becoming uncertain. Your marriage or relationship is coming to an end. Your financial situation is going to change. And you have many financial questions. Will you have enough income? Will you be able to stay in your house? Will your children be able to go to college? So a low-cost attorney would easily catch your eye. And, we all like to save money. No one wants to pay too much for something. But you get what you pay for.

Some law firms charge less because they make up for it in volume. They have a stable of inexperienced attorneys who will handle your case, and get it settled as quickly as possible. They don't invest enough of their time. Do they get you a settlement? Yes. Is it something you can live with? Maybe.

Remember, experience matters. People who choose inexperienced, lower-priced attorneys in family law cases often lose out. They lose out financially. They lose out on custody of their children. Often, their attorneys miss out on opportunities or can't take advantage of them. Many times, people think they have a simple, uncomplicated case....so why can't they save money on their attorney?

But what if their spouse or partner hires an experienced attorney? Suddenly a simple case can turn complicated...and the couple isn't on the same playing field. When you're dealing with your future and your family's future, value is much more important than price.

At the Law Offices of Vincent W. Davis and Associates, we see many clients who have been burned by price shopping. They come to us to try to repair the damage. Unfortunately, sometimes it's too late.

Does Vince charge more per hour than some attorneys? Yes. But every hour he spends on you gives you the benefit of his 28 years of experience as an attorney - his extensive experience in family law - his courtroom experience of more than 200 family law trials.

Our clients look at it as an investment...one that pays off with financial security and peace of mind.

And by the way, the difference in price is usually much less than people think. There are times to go to Costco....and times when saving a few dollars can cost you a lot more. When choosing a family law attorney, choose the best you can afford - which is oftentimes more than you might expect.

Mistake 6: Not Using an Attorney

This chapter actually contains several mistakes - mistakes that are very easy to make here in California. Very easy, but very costly.

First, many people assume that because California makes divorce "very simple", they don't always need separate attorneys...or even an attorney at all. Others think because they live together but aren't married, they shouldn't bother with an attorney, because they don't have the same rights as a spouse.

And some people whose divorce is final believe because their case is over, they shouldn't get an attorney to try to change or correct something they're having trouble living with.

All three assumptions are wrong. All three are costly. They cost people money. They cost parents custody of their children.

Take the first one. Yes, California has laws on the books to simplify divorce. But when couples use the same attorney, there isn't anyone looking out for each side individually. And, when they try to save money by using a paralegal instead of an attorney, or doing it themselves, that's when mistakes happen. Things get overlooked.

For example, a shift in housing prices, or stock prices, or the value of other assets can have a huge impact on a financial settlement. And suddenly things aren't so simple anymore.

An experienced family law attorney is always watching out for his client, and knows what to be on the lookout for.

What about couples who aren't married? We certainly see high-profile and celebrity cases in the news all the time. And while their lifestyle is a lot different than yours, their issues are often the same.

Child custody and visitation, and child support. These issues can actually be more complicated when the parents were never married. Maybe one parent is now living with someone new. Maybe a parent takes a child for a weekend and never brings him or her back. And many parents wrongly believe they'll have to settle for what they can get, not get what they want.

Unfortunately, too many attorneys steer them in that direction.

Then there are couples who are divorced. Maybe they have been for a few years. And things are different now. Their children are older. They have different needs. The custody arrangement might not be working out. Child support may no longer be sufficient, because lifestyles change.

One spouse might have remarried. Gotten a better job, or lost their job. And, the last thing someone who's gone through a divorce wants is to hire another attorney and go back to court.

But even though that divorce is a legal agreement, a good attorney can help fix what's broken. At the Law Offices of Vincent W. Davis and Associates, we've done that....for people in all three of these categories.

Remember, mistakes are easy to make. Repairing the damage is a lot harder.

Mistake 7: Forgetting You're the Client

Customer service. We expect it in a store. We're the customer. We're spending our money. And we could be spending it somewhere else. There's plenty of competition. It should be just as important when you're choosing a family law attorney. In fact, more so.

This may be the most difficult time in your life. A relationship is coming to an end. A family is coming apart. Your lives won't be the same.

And, the last thing you need is to feel that your case just isn't very important to your attorney - that you aren't very important. Unfortunately, this complaint is all too common in the legal profession.

People say once they've chosen their attorney,

they feel like they've disappeared into a black hole. There's no communication. No updates. No calls or emails. Even their own calls don't get returned, or if they do it's not in a timely fashion. This may be common, but it certainly isn't right.

You're dealing with difficult issues - and not just legal issues. Practical issues...like finances. Will you be able to pay your bills on time, or at all? Emotional issues. . . Will you be okay? This is a very challenging and very personal time for anyone.

Sometimes just hearing a voice or getting an email or text can make all the difference. For too many attorneys, clients are just that. Clients – cases - not people. That perception can start with the very first consult.

It can be brief. Or the attorney can do a lot of talking and very little listening. And once that first consult is over, some clients don't see their attorney again for months. They deal with associates or paralegals or other people in the office, until their case goes to trial, or is settled. And they get a bill.

When you're choosing a family law attorney, be sure to ask about service. What's their policy? How do they treat their clients? How will they treat you?

We take this very seriously at the Law Offices of Vincent W. Davis and Associates. We know how important it is to you, so it's just as important to us.

In fact, Vince gives every one of his clients his cellphone number. How many attorneys do that? He gets dozens of calls and texts every day. And while he may not be able to take a call or call back in a timely fashion, he can text. And he does - sometimes within seconds.

Since client emails go right to his phone, he can respond to them quickly as well. And it's not just Vince. Everyone in the firm....other attorneys, legal staff, secretaries and receptionists....know how important you are, and how important service is.

It can be an inconvenience to get a call or text or email at odd hours. But what our clients are going through is far more than an inconvenience. These events are changing their lives. And your case doesn't watch the clock. Important questions and concerns don't just come up during regular office hours.

Communication. Service. That's what you deserve. And you deserve an attorney who provides them.

Peace of Mind from the Law Offices of Vincent W. Davis and Associates

We know we've given you a lot to think about. There's a lot of information in this guide. And a lot of it is complicated.

But so is life.

Especially when your life is changing. And, if you're in need of a family law attorney, your life could be changing dramatically....and becoming a lot more complicated. And there's a lot at stake – like your financial needs, and your emotional needs.

The decisions you make now will affect you and your family for years to come. . .beginning with your choice of lawyer. Make the right choice and you get more than an attorney...you get an advocate. One who fights for you, and goes into the battle armed with experience, knowledge, and skills.

Divorce Secrets

Too many people don't have the information they need to make the right choice....and they end up paying the price. The Law Offices of Vincent W. Davis and Associates have fought...and won...for people, throughout Southern California, for nearly 30 years.

People going through what you're going through now. . .people who were in the biggest fight of their lives. We hope you'll give us the chance to fight for you. Just call 888-888-6582 to book your "fighting for your family" consultation.

Protect yourself.
Your children.
Your assets.
Your rights.

www.ingramcontent.com/pod-product-compliance
Lightning Source LLC
Chambersburg PA
CBHW041118180526
45172CB00001B/305